A NEW LIGHT IN METAPHYSICS

Alejandro Martínez Castillo
Salto
Uruguay
2025/September

AMAZON
www.amazon.com
ISBN: 9798667531531

QUOTES:

"I believe in God but my God does have problems. If not God would have already solved everything."

"There exist two mountains, the Physics Sciences' one and the Religions' one. Between, a valley to transit."

PHILOSOPHIC PRINCIPLES

"The purpose of the existence is to enjoy life and if we can't, we can think and work to make it possible."

"Everything must make sense in the Universe and if something doesn't is because we haven't understood it properly or because there's something wrong."

"One thing is how things should be; other is how they really are."

"Sometimes we don't see what we are not looking for..."

"Sometimes we don't see what we don't want to see..."

REALITY IS HARD

All kind of diseases, calamities, catastrophes and tragedies... We don't live in any Paradise. But not being human beings' fault, what fails is the Physics of the Universe.

Nowadays organic molecules "break" causing mutations, cancer, cells' deterioration, aging and death. A more ideal kind of life should exist.

Some physics-parameters could have a wrong real running value, some physical things could not be exactly the way they should be and the Universe could be in a not ideal state. Nature could be different.

The Physics of the Universe determines everything material and the entire Nature itself including our own organism. Failing, the things are not as they should be. And in this are all of us, living a wrong life from which nobody escapes.

What remains for us is try to live the better possible way doing what we know and could do that always, in one way or another, ends being something others are needing. Nothing else remains.

Our Universe seems to have not born perfect. Something could have gone wrong in its creation.

Hope would exist if some "God", capable to fix the flaw, would exist.

But that God could have also been affected and have troubles...

May be we, all humans at Earth, could help someway just following our intuition. Every thing we could solve here could help God solve something there. Everything could be important.

That's what makes sense to me. That's my faith.

LOGICAL PROOF OF A CREATOR GOD

Elementary particles exist in the Universe with laws of their interaction and behavior.

The possible interactions are like attractions and repulsions and are determined by the concept of forces.

All are "action at a distance" forces. This means that a "Physics Machine" would exist "running" the Physics Laws on the elementary particles.

This leaves us to think in a mathematically based Universe that would "run" in some kind of "Universal Supra-Computer".

The proof of the existence of a creator God follows quite obviously:

Some kind of "Superior Intelligence" must have defined the elementary particles and programmed the Physics Laws with their particular constants' values that unavoidably run over the particles.

That intelligence must also have determined the way for the particles to appear in the Universe.

That "Superior Intelligence" can be called the "Universe's God".

Of course the questions on how a "Universal Supra-Computer" and the "Universe's God" could come into existence arise but that is another story.

The reasoning here proves the existence of a creator God, not how came into existence.

It is also not presented here any other possible capability of the Universe's God particularly in which way God could observe and intervene in his creation.

THE WISE AND GOD

_ *Wise, about life... Too much bad things happen...*

_ *Seems this is a wrong kind of life. Our World seems to be fortuitous. Is not as it is supposed a World and life would be. The things are not as they should be.*

_ *Wise, God created the Universe, how would exist something wrong?*

_ *God could have got own troubles...*

_ *But God would have all power to solve anything... What would be missing to solve the things?*

_ *Nobody knows God's situation. There's no way to communicate with God. Who knows...*

_ *Nothing that could be done about...*

_ *One thing is true, if there is a God with a creation God must have a way to perceive it, may be through our own eyes and ears. So God could observe us and may be someone could imagine something useful for God to solve the things. Every thing we could solve here could help God solve something there.*

May be God could guide our intuition to something...

Just maybe...

May be also could be just a matter of time...

That's what I think...

SPECULATIONS ON PROBLEMS OF LIFE, THE UNIVERSE AND GOD

IDEAL LIFE

Nothing wrong and or bad must exist in an ideal kind of life. A totally enjoyable, comfortable and safe life to live:

_ Animals eating fruits, seeds and leafs from vegetables only. That must be enough.

_ All beings respecting all other beings. Not damaging any other being.

_ No diseases at all.

_ No tragedies, no catastrophes at all.

_ No aging, no natural death. Births and possible deaths would be extraordinary events only.

WRONG PHYSICS PARAMETERS' VALUES

At the "Reality is hard" page is argued that the Physics parameters' values would not be the ideal ones as they should be.

If they were ideal, ideal kinds of life would exist on ideal planets as described above.

Assuming that God didn't plan the Universe and the life in it the way they are, God's specifications of the parameters' values would not be the current ones. Wrong parameter's values in reality different from the specified ones can only be explained by the "Physics' Machine" of the Universe, running all the Physics Laws of the Universe, flawing someway.

POSSIBLE FLAW

The Universe is huge and a too huge one would mean too much things to be processed at the same time what could have exceeded the capacity of the "Physics' Machine" to process all the Physics' data at a proper time.

A too large delaying in the processing time implies a slower timing in the Physics of the Universe what would have the same effect of altering the Physics parameters' values.

In other words the flaw would consist in an overloading of the main "Physics' Machine" by a Universe that was too big since the beginnings in its creation.

GOD AND SYSTEMS SITUATION

The bad state of Life in the Universe for so long time can only be explained if also God and God's systems have been affected seriously by the problems in their own Physics.

If not God would have already solved everything long time ago.

MAY BE:

If our Universe is a creation, of God must have a way to perceive it and it would be through our own eyes, ears and other senses. So God could observe us and may be someone could imagine something useful for God to solve the things.

Every thing we could solve here could help God solve something there. Everything could be important.

May be we, all humans at Earth, with all of our developed knowledge, technology and imagination could help someway just following our intuition.

That's what makes sense to me.

That's my faith.

JUST A POSSIBILITY

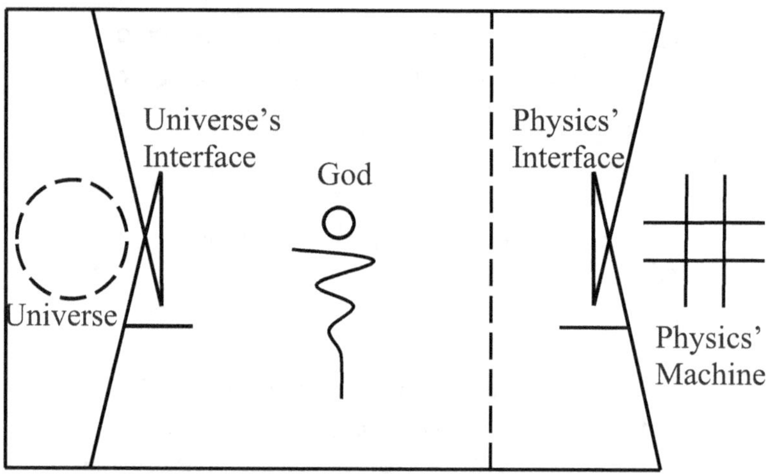

The "Physics' Machine" runs all Physics Laws at the same time. The God's Physics Laws and the Universe's Physics Laws.

God's Physics Laws would let be God's body and his environment in which there would be an Interface to the "Physics' Machine" and an Interface to manage the Universe. The first one would let God develop and setup all Physics Laws even his own ones. The second one would let God create some things in the Universe and observe it connecting to beings' minds perceiving for instance what they are seeing and hearing. God specifies both, the Universe and himself.

What I could imagine that can make sense to me is that, due to its own Physics' problems, God acquired amnesia at the beginning of the Universe about everything before and even about himself.

God would be considering then now, to be just some "Manager" of the Universe and that there would be a yet "Superior Intelligence" responsible for it.

God would have been waiting then, for his intervention for so long.

God not aware of being God...

Thinking in a possible way God could solve the things is having access to the "Physics' Interface".

It could be hiding by some entire wall which could vanish some way.

For instance, the wall could vanish by touching something in it in some special way like the touching force, timing, etc.

It must be noted that the physics' problems could make the things worse and something could be not working fine.

The complex problem then now could reside in how God would look for something God would be thinking would not be the case.

The problem of course is expected to be complex, if it wasn't, it would have already been solved time ago.

If the situation described here would be right and God could get aware of it some way, he could be able to think in something that would let him finally solve all the things.

God would be able to know about a possible situation he would not be taking into consideration and be able to solve some problems he would not be aware about.

NOTE:

This is just a possibility.

May be other ways God could be in problems for so long, since the beginnings, could be imagined.
This is one I could imagine that could make sense to me.

My hope is that it could help God solve the problems.

If right, it could be just a matter of time for everything be finally solved.

If wrong or something is missing, it would at least be useful to inspire someone else to find the right one or what is missing what would be also just a matter of time.

It must be pointed out that time could be needed for this possibility to be properly taken in consideration by God and time could be needed for some things to be accomplished.

In one way or another we all could help someway just following our intuition. Every time we solve something here it could help God solve something there.

That's my faith...

A PHRASE AND A PAGE FOR RELIGIONS IN PEACE

The phrase:

"God could have troubles and maybe we could help some way."

The page:

"Reality is hard"

(Challenging things of Religions and things of Science of course)

If religions would have them into account they would stay in peace each one looking in an own way for the problems God could have and how a help could be given because they would be the real cause that prevents him from setting up the new promised world.

A matter of real faith...

NOTE:

A main subject in Religions is which, and in which ways, "souls" ("minds") could be saved for a "New World" their God(s) would setup at some time. This subject is not covered here in this manuscript. It is leaved to Religions to treat that subject on their own way.

The aim in this manuscript is to treat what would be missing for the setup of a "New World" and for it to happen once for all.